Der J

1

EVERYONE
NEEDS A
HERO

When I wrote this book,
I didn't think something
like this could happen...
Someone reads it... an interview
from the Hero's friend
I connect... I started
writing this a year ago...
Can't say that someone
like you was on my
mind then...

like this could happen...

I don't know what God has in store,

EVERYONE NEEDS A HERO

WHY CAN'T IT BE YOU?

but I know YOU are worthy, beautiful, & deserve the world. You're a Hero Jasmyn,

THANK YOU For Being You!!

AIMÉ MUKENDI, JR.
@SIRAIMÉZING aka "Boo"

Everyone Needs A Hero: Why Can't It Be You?

Copyright © 2020 Aimé Mukendi, Jr. Aka "Sir Aimézing"

BMD Publishing
All Rights Reserved

ISBN # 979-8628292044

BMDPublishing@MarketDominationLLC.com
MarketDominationLLC.com

BMD Publishing CEO: Seth Greene
Editorial Management: Bruce Corris
Layout & Cover Creation: Kristin Watt

Salah Qamachi photography

DEDICATIONS

This book is dedicated to everyone who ever felt inadequate, lonely or insecure. To anyone who ever looked in the mirror and asked, "Why was I created?" This volume was written to inspire, educate and motivate the power that lies within every single one of us roaming planet Earth.

I was a kid who got called soft, ugly, stupid and whose crushes and feelings for girls were never reciprocated. I was a kid who searched for a feeling of acceptance and wanted to feel cool in a world where people act like cool has only one definition. I was a kid who used to look in the mirror and feel insufficient. I was a kid who contemplated suicide.

On this journey, I've battled demons daily.

My goal is to use that pain and those struggles to help. If that wasn't my duty, then I wouldn't be here. My best advice is that if I can do it, you can do it.

PREFACE

Thank you for reading and embarking on this journey with me. You have a story to share and a talent that can change our world forever.

It's inside of you. My only aim was to spark that flame through these words.

I'm an introvert who's become a speaker and an instrument of light to help the world. You can be more introverted than me, but I've learned how to be less introverted.

I'm comfortable with this now. Learning everyday.

I'm a very shy person but I've learned to be more outgoing. I'm probably more introverted than extroverted, sometimes people think I'm lying. When I get excited the introvert goes away.

My job is to help people discover their greatness. The hero within.

I'm Aimé. Someone once called me, "Sir Aimézing" and every day I'm trying to live up to that name. I've been able to turn my dreams into reality amidst adversity.

The reason this resonates with you is because every life has adversity. Everyone needs to dig deeper and find their grit. My story is one more reminder that if you set your mind to it and commit, you can do it.

#ShiftupwithSir

TABLE OF CONTENTS

DEMONS

DEMONS
THE DAY I DIED AND LIVED TO TELL ABOUT IT

Being President of a Non-Profit organization requires a lot of attention. Especially when you're in the beginning stages and looking to cultivate a team, dedicated to the mission. It was a beautiful pre-summer day and I was excited because after months of struggling to adjust our schedules and finding the "right time," our group was finally able to meet. Everyone was present. We had a diverse squad. A party-planner, a successful salesman, an educator, a mentor and connector, a visionary with years of music industry experience, a newly graduated finance major and me.

Each individual was hand-picked because of their skills, upbringing and passion for our youth. We were a team focused and locked in looking to help. However, on that day, I was called to help sooner than I could have ever imagined. There are members of our original board who may never know this until they read this book. Mid-meeting my phone flashed with a notification. It was my ex. When I opened the text, I saw an alarming message in all CAPS. I ended the meeting abruptly. No one questioned and no one knew what was happening.

Being madly in love with someone who is toxic has cost many people their lives. Some live to share their story, others live through hell and some are dead. Memorial Day had just passed and even though we both knew that we should have accepted going separate ways, the magnet of our lust found us once again playing the same old game.

That Monday as we drove to her house, I had no idea what would happen in the near future. I'll never forget because she was singing a song by French Montana:

Even though the world was meant for you

I hope you don't get famous

'Cause everyone will love you but won't love you

like the way I do, oh nah

Hope you don't get famous (Hope you don't get famous)

Stay home with me

Stay home with me

I'll always love ya, I'll always

Hope you don't get

Hope you don't get famous

Hope you don't get famous

Hope you don't get famous

I must admit. When she sang those lyrics it seemed like a movie. Fast forward to my first official scholarship meeting.

My ex-girlfriend texted me and I ran to her rescue. There was a man there, and he and I engaged in an altercation. I beat the guy up. He then quickly points a gun at me. He subsequently pointed the gun at my head and in that moment, I stepped up to it and dared him to shoot me.

He pulls the trigger.

The police department examined the weapon and there was nothing wrong with it.

It should've been fired.

I should've been dead.

The medical examiner said that the bullet, fired into my skull at point blank range, would have killed me, but I know better.

Even though the gun didn't go off, I died that day, and I lived to tell about it.

I believe that I was saved from a physical death, so that I could die spiritually and be reborn for a higher purpose. I'm here today to share with you what killed me, what saved me, what died in me and how you don't have to die to experience the same transformation that I did.

I'll never forget talking with my mom when she looked me in the face and said, "All men cheat." I don't know if she realized what she really was saying to me. I don't think she knew those words would stick with me forever. I don't think she knew that hearing those words from the most important woman in my life fueled an ego that eventually led to me having a gun pointed at my head at age 26.

Radio personality Charlamagne said this on his show *The Breakfast Club*, "Men cheat because of ego; Women cheat because of emo." This quote resonated and piled on the foundation my mother had already laid. This sentiment defined what it means to be a man, or the idea that plagues so many men just like me. When you grow up in a household where men never treat your mother right, or go to sleep hearing your mother scream as a man abuses her, you start to grow a shell.

I can remember the fear that filled my heart at night, hearing my mother in pain as items were knocked to the floor, and she was pushed and thrust into walls. I've never written about this. The echo of her frightened yelp haunted me at night. That anxiety created a hysteria in me.

I was a gangly 13 year old with a scratchy voice, who as he waited for the bus, watched a man scream and hold my mother against our front door. After all the nights of hearing her scared cries, all the days of seeing her tears, and all the moments of witnessing my mother be abused, belittled and hurt, I tried to be a hero.

I knew there wasn't much I could do, but there was something inside me that raged to help. I ran over to this man, Stacey -- whom at the time I hated -- yanked his shoulder and held his stare as he grabbed me in return by my collar and tossed me across the living room.

That moment, I said to myself, "Never again." I didn't challenge that man physically ever again. But that moment changed me forever. There came a time when my mother, my brother and I had to leave our house. We stayed with my Godmother, my mother's friend whom I will love forever. Even though I was getting a ride to my suburban school from the city and our living situation had changed, no one at my school ever knew. Not one peer, teacher or counselor.

I never shared with anyone that school was my peace. My sanctuary. My opportunity to run away from the dangers of my home life. To be honest, I don't think my dad ever knew my mother was being abused, and that I, the oldest son, had to stomach and watch it.

My mother didn't have me young, but it felt like it was us against the world. When she and my father split, we had to leave the apartment we lived in and she had to work two jobs.

Sometimes we stayed with my great-grandparents and my grandmother. There were even nights we stayed at the City Mission until she could get back on her feet.

I teared up writing this. Mom, I hope you know how much I love you. I didn't forget and I never will.

My mother made things happen. She raised me to be a warrior. She taught me to be accountable and understand that as a man, I would need to be responsible. I was in every way shape and form, a "Mama's boy." And I knew in order to be a hero to my mom, I had to get good grades and have good behavior.

Have you ever been in love before? Not with a person, but with your ego? You become so deeply invested in the image you want the world to see and obsessed with the idea of invincibility and perfection. When you grow up an African American male, there really is no definition of what it means to be a man. Unfortunately, that often means when African Americans are put in leadership positions, we fall flat on our faces.

Growing up, I tried to absorb bits and pieces from all the men around me. Television, music and sports figures were my heroes. LeBron James, Kanye West and Will Smith were the men I dreamed of emulating. Cliff Huxtable, Uncle Phil and James Evans were the father figures I hoped to become.

My name is Aimé Mukendi, Jr., but many times in my life I felt so far from my father, it meant nothing. When you grow up in the Hip-Hop/NBA culture, you start to measure success and fulfillment in material items. I grew up in an era where Bow Wow, Romeo and all the other "Lils" had everything we all wanted. They had fame, bought their mothers houses and caught the eye of every girl.

That's what I wanted. That's what I dreamed of.

There are some things that happened to me before the age of 13 that changed my life. Too many times we discount our childhoods and situations that ultimately come out of us when we get into the real world.

I remember having a crush on my pre-K teacher. She was a brunette, with an average face and slim build. I couldn't tell you her name. I couldn't tell you if she was actually attractive. I can only say that at four years old, I knew she had something I wanted. Is that how little creeps are formed in America? Kid can't get an erection, but knows when a woman is sexy. It's actually kind of scary because that was the 90s.

One day it was nap time. My mother worked part-time at my Pre-K to ensure nothing happened to me. I'm not sure where she was on this day. The teacher laid me down on my mat as her job required, but somehow, I finagled my hand up the teacher's sleeve and rubbed her entire arm.

At four years old, in a way or form, I was sexually assaulting women. Chilling as that may be, the disgusting fact tells a bigger story of not only myself but the culture in our world.

When I was five or six, my mother had a friend who babysat me. At the time, my mother had to work multiple jobs to do what was needed to get by and create a better life for me. One afternoon, after my babysitter fed me and let me watch some TV, she decided to take a nap.

When she took this nap, she removed her pants. I can still remember to this day seeing a brown-skinned black woman, wearing a scarf, white shirt and panties. She lay next to me under the covers on the living room floor of the apartment. Her back towards me, I touched her. I spooned with a grown woman and I enjoyed it. For some reason people think children are unaware. Looking back now it makes me uneasy. I'm not sure what to call this situation. She didn't touch me, but she did expose her body in a way that impacted my reaction.

In second grade, I had a new babysitter. She was one of the sweetest women I ever knew.

She looked out for me and my mother. After school, she'd pick me up in her blue van and take me to her house. She always made sure I ate and that my homework was done. My heart warms up when I think about her. She stood out because she had a speech impediment and some sort of walking disability. Noble souls adopt children, and she adopted a girl who was in 5th grade, who was older than me. I don't think she ever knew what happened between me and her daughter. Every time we were together, we fondled each other. Groping and touching our underdeveloped bodies, we stuck our hands down each other's pants constantly. Every single day. Monday-Friday, it was homework and hand action.

Often her mother was just in the neighboring room oblivious to our sexual encounters. There were times when we would jump back fast as she walked into the room.

The irony of life is that she came with my older cousin as

his plus-one to Thanksgiving a few years back. We didn't make much contact, but something in my heart tells me she remembers.

By the time I was 10 years old, I was hanging out with more girls. It was during the summer and I was making out with a 15-year-old girl in the pool. In addition I was whipping out my dick and flashing everyone, I even humped girls. At 10 years old, I may have been getting more action than the average adult!

It's scary to think about what a child can have access to in our modern world. All during these encounters, I was an only-child for most of my life, whose mother loved him dearly, sacrificed and did all she could to protect me. She made sure I had a relationship with the creator, dressed me well, and fed me. When I was seven years old, she bought her first home, laying a foundation for a strong upbringing.

She is my hero.

I never went into detail about these situations because worse things have happened to better people. And I never wanted to cause anymore pain for my mother. "A wise son makes a glad father, but a foolish son is the grief of his mother."- Proverbs 10:1. When I told my dad about this book, he told me how proud he was. Sharing these stories with my mother would have put me in the same boat as the man who put his hands on her. I never wanted to add to her pain. My mother shared so much of her story with me and told me of the countless times people took advantage of her. At age 15, my mother was raped by an ex-boyfriend of my late grandmother. He currently is serving a life sentence for a double-homicide in California.

Sharing this with her wouldn't make me a hero. That isn't what a man would do.

So how can one become both? The plague in my community is that men measure women as stats. Women are numbers and the trophy of a sport. Step into any barbershop, cafeteria or locker room and the conversation of "How many girls..." still resonates. It played along with what I encompassed as success: earning fame, buying my mother a house and having countless women. These childhood experiences fueled me as I grew up.

By the time I got to college, I was lanky and my shell of an ego bled into every aspect of my life.

"My ego is my imaginary friend

He was with me when I was only imagining

I had dreams of the league

One day I play Kobe

I walk up to Puff and he already know me

Coulda let the dream killers kill my self esteem

Or use the arrogance as a steam that powers my dreams

And my ego"

– Kanye West

As a college freshman in August, I stood 6'1, 185 lbs. By May the following year, I was 225 lbs, solid muscle. Built like an NFL running back so no man could ever toss me like a burnt-out cigarette butt again, my armor added another layer of ego. A layer that changed me forever.

Heroes can't be bullied. Heroes can't be taken advantage of. Heroes protect their mothers and more. I fell in love with my ego, but I hated myself.

I wrote this in June 2018 at age 25:

At this stage I'm constantly relying on weed and alcohol to fill the void of not having a girlfriend, but truly I work to fill an even deeper lack of self-love.

How does one be single when he doesn't want to be?

I've been asking myself this question for so long. How do I find this inner-love that the world so eloquently depicts? A land filled with humans clawing and biting for the same things:

Satisfaction, Acceptance, Completeness.

It's like we're all just bodies flowing and moving about. Witherless and ignorant to all the madness surrounding us. Our innocence fades each day as we grow into vessels just reaching for the infinite.

This is the beginning of my self-entitled biography. Maybe not. Only time will tell...

Why do I think you all should call me sir? Because I'm a cocky a**hole who from time to time likes my ego stroked? Yes. But, it's just plain and simply respectful. The most respectful way to address a man is to call him sir. Likewise for women it should be miss, ma'am, and madam. I'm just built differently. Sometimes I catch myself in my thoughts.

I usually get lost. Do you know what that's like? Looking in a mirror and seeing a blank, unfamiliar being? You're trying to find your identity, but it's like you're on a chase.

Literally, like one of those crazy illuminati movies with computers and spies chasing White guys dressed in black.

You're walking the path with no GPS. You just have opportunities to look back and see a few things you remember. Then you're in the middle of the coliseum and three lions are charging at you.

It's either them or you.

And that's life.

The irony of those words I wrote was that I had no idea what would be in store for me just under a year later. You already know the ending of this story, but I want to go into more detail about just what happened on that fateful day.

May 29, 2019:

It was the first time we had our entire board present for a meeting to fundraise for our inaugural scholarship. During the meeting, I received a phone call. I wasn't able to answer it, but I quickly took a look at my phone and saw a text message in all CAPS. It was my ex-girlfriend alerting me that her daughter's father was trying to break into her house.

I ended the meeting. Jumped in my car. Took off my chain and put on my cape. I ran red lights. I cut cars off. I thought I was Batman. Upon arrival the joker was not on site.

He would return.

During the time I waited for him to come back, a group of students gathered outside the house, gearing up to fight. One of the students knew me from some of the community work I do. He was a part of a project that surveys young men on healthy masculinity. My ex and I worked to stop these students from fighting. In fact, I held a young man back as he begged me to let him go so he could justifiably defend himself.

That's when a white sedan pulled up. I saw the man who terrorized the woman I loved get out of the car. Without hesitation I ran over to him. We tussled in the middle of the street. He had a friend with him, but I needed no help. I brutally punched, kicked and brawled with him in the street.

Neighbors watched as my ego took over, and I bashed the face of another Black man. After my ex's screams and his friend's attempt to end the scuffle, my opponent went to the back of the car and grabbed a pistol. I can't describe the gun. All I remember is that he pointed it at my forehead.

"Shoot me. I dare you." I said with no consideration for either the children watching or the witnessing neighbors.

I didn't think about my mother. My sister. My teenage brother. My nephew. My baby brother. I didn't think of all the people who had believed in me, and had gone out of their way to help me through life. I didn't think about the students I was facilitating and helping define what it means to be a man and be masculine.

The only thing fueling me at this moment was ego.

I wanted to die a "hero."

He pulled the trigger.

Moments later, more than 20 police cars were on site apprehending him. I hugged the children that once called him Daddy and apologized for having them see me act in such a way. As we finished police reports, officers confirmed that the pistol was loaded. Had the gun locked?

Misfired?

I will never know.

In the coming weeks, I struggled with the question of why I lived. In early June, I wrote this, which captured my emotional roller coaster:

"The emotions I have going through this process are indescribable. I feel used. I feel hurt. I feel like a victim of a physical, mental and emotional crime. I've began to believe I was set-up. My faith in GOD won't allow me to dip too low. Job lost and everything and didn't fold, neither can I."

May 29, 2019 I stared death in its face, and not because I loved anyone or anything other than my own ego. Did that make me a man?

No. It was at this moment I realized why I survived. It was at this moment that I knew everything had to change.

PURPOSE

PURPOSE

Purpose is what dictates the emotions and the existence of so many elements of life. Think about it -- when you're a kid and you hit somebody too hard, what's the first thing you say besides, "I'm sorry" when you get in trouble?

You change the pitch of your voice, tap into the baby version of yourself so that there's a pretend innocence in your eye and say, "I didn't do it on purpose!"

This justification of violating our neighbors doesn't change in adulthood. Just the words we use to describe it does. When you're in a relationship and you cheat on your partner it's, "I didn't mean to." Translation: PURPOSE!

What separates a person from happiness versus going through the motions of life?

PURPOSE!

Every ship that sails has a purpose, a destination. What makes people think we are any different from a ship? We may not live in water directly, but water is a necessity for every element of our existence. From survival to hygiene, there will never be a time where we, as humans, like a ship do not depend on water.

However, more importantly, a human without a purpose, destination or goal will drift. Just like a ship without a captain.

Think about it. Ships go through storms, unexpected challenging situations where it seems like it's all coming to an end, all on the voyage to their destination.

Life is like the sea. Why do you think they always say, "There are plenty more fish in the sea." Because our world is filled with humans floating with no guidance or purpose. Just drifting.

So how do we find our way?

In my case, it was to bite off more than I could chew.

Stepping into a room with people who have access to enough money to change the world is a really humbling experience. You feel the urge to brag that you're with these types of people, but simultaneously you also figure out the right way to approach the heavy hitters.

For me, communication is something learned, not innate. I'm actually extremely shy. As a kid, I said very few words to strangers or anyone who I wasn't comfortable with. Today, as a person who has a niche in networking, public speaking and marketing, it's interesting to think about.

So how? What did it take to create who the world knows as Sir Aimézing?

Prayer, Failure and Reading.

And it all started with PURPOSE.

There was always a higher purpose for me. I've told you some of my secrets, and now it's time to talk about how I didn't let them hold me back. What does it feel like to chase your dream? To know the train is in front of you waiting for you to board and you have the power to pick the destination? I've never felt more alive.

There are millions who never attempt to become their own master. They rely on experts for every facet of life. They turn not just to the Instagram speakers, YouTubers or seminar organizers. They look for experts in colleagues, friends and family.

Is that your approach? Do you let others influence your ultimate decisions? This is a book for people looking to SHIFT UP! A book for people who fully understand and truly want to change their lives.

No man can create change without first changing himself.

WRITE DOWN YOUR GOALS

WRITE DOWN YOUR GOALS

In July 2018, I met with an advisor who told me it was necessary to write out my goals. Grab a pen and paper, and do the same.

There are three categories:

1. Personal
2. Financial
3. Spiritual

For brainstorming purposes I will share what I wrote back then.

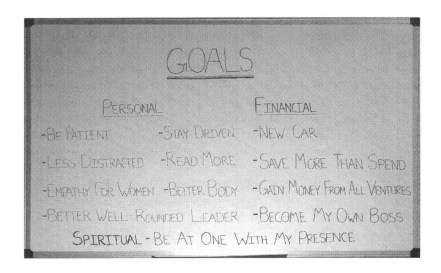

Personal:

-Be Patient
-Stay Driven
-Less Distracted
-Read More
-Better Body
-Better Well-Rounded Leader
-Empathy for Women

Financial:

-New Car
-Save More than Spend
-Gain Money from All Ventures
-Become My Own Boss

Spiritual:

-Be at One with my Presence.

What's your list? It's impossible to match mine. And before you second-guess yourself...

*"If a doubt comes to you,
cast it away as sin."*

– Wallace D. Wattles

These goals won't mean a thing if you don't adjust your character and behavior.

Do you like counting Benjamins? I certainly do. I've never frowned while having some in my hand, except for when I had to give them to my landlord. But, a different kind of Benjamin opened my eyes to my flaws and helped me become better. I implemented a practice of following the example of Ben Franklin, one of our country's founding fathers.

Ben Franklin's 13 Virtues.

Every Monday on my *@SirAimezing* Instagram story, I share my "Word of the Week" all based on principles that Franklin listed to help develop his character.

1. **Temperance:** abstinence from alcoholic drink. Eat not to dullness: drink not to elevation. Through college and up until the start of 2019, liquor was my go-to. Life was just better with a little bit of sauce. Yes, this includes wine. In addition to putting this word in my mind for a week, throughout the week I made sure I read Bible verses that included this idea in its text. I'll share one: Proverbs 31:4-5 "It is not for kings, O Lemuel, It is not for kings to drink wine, Nor for princes intoxicating drink; Lest they drink and forget the law, And pervert the justice of all afflicted."

Why implement this? "Alcohol is legal and sometimes I just want to loosen up after a long day or week." That is a dependency that ultimately holds every single one of us back. Alcohol is a depressant, so even though it makes us feel good, it can be a crutch and another way to distract us from achieving a goal. Through college and up until the start of 2019, liquor was my answer.

Yet, I discovered the discipline of going weeks at a time without even a single glass of wine. Don't get me wrong, some of my most creative nights have come with a glass of wine, Apple Music and a poster board. However, going through this discipline added another level of grit. Keep my eyes on the target.

There's another bonus this brings. When you're a single Aquarius who enjoys a woman's touch, not drinking makes things run a lot smoother. You can't send a drunk text if you don't get drunk.

One last note: I suggest you go to a networking event, happy hour or any type of function around people. When someone asks, "Would you like a drink" ask for water or cranberry juice. Don't even drink a beer and watch how taken aback people become. It's extremely intriguing to stand out. But, most importantly, you are maintaining control.

2. **Silence:** Speak not but what may benefit others or yourself; avoid trifling conversation. Complete absence of sound. Verse: James 1:19 "My dear brothers and sisters, take note of this: Everyone should be quick to listen, slow to speak and slow to become angry." (NIV)

I'm outspoken. Headstrong. Hardheaded. And I've made plenty of mistakes when it comes to saying too many words. Don't believe me, ask one of my exes…

There are a few things we gain by remaining silent. We can observe. Study the people around us. Examine the interactions. There will always be someone who says too much and those words can cost you opportunities or money and ultimately prolong you from your goals. Always say less than necessary. On a weekly basis this was good practice because I trained my mind and body to anticipate instead of react. Life is about preparation. Not being prepared can be the difference between being seen as a hero or a villain, especially when it comes to words.

3. **Order:** Let all your things have their places; let each part of your business have its time. The arrangement or disposition of people or things in relation to each other according to a particular sequence, pattern or method. 1 Timothy 3:4 "He must be one who manages his own household well, keeping his children under control with all dignity."(NASB)

Order is defined as the arrangement or disposition of people or things in relation to each other according to a particular sequence, pattern or method. Having a set routine, or specific way of doing things only enhances the tedious effort it takes to gain success. There's not a successful person who's ever roamed the planet who didn't have some type of order. For me, it included cleaning, business tasks, organizing my calendar, but most importantly, how I carried myself. Can't be in order if I'm scrolling through Instagram. Can't be in order if I'm not available to give my little brother advice.

4. **Resolution:** Resolve to perform what you ought; perform without fail what you resolve. A firm decision to do or not to do something. James 1:25 "But the one who looks intently into the perfect law of freedom and continues in it-not forgetting what they have heard, but doing it-they will be blessed in what they do." (NIV)

I always knew it was going to be a great week when this word popped up. It meant that whatever issues, whether relationships, finances or emotions, by the end of the week GOD was going to provide me the solution to the problem. It was encouraging. Most associate this word with the New Year. We all are happy at the beginning of the year. Optimism fills our land and the fake gym-goers are ready bright and early for three weeks in January. But it's not a once a year idea. It's continuous and just by thinking about this word daily, my week flows smoother.

5. **Frugality:** Make no expense but do good to others or yourself; i.e.waste nothing. The quality of being economical with money or food; thriftiness Proverbs 21:20 "There is precious treasure and oil in the dwelling of the wise, but a foolish man swallows it."

Frugality. Cheap. Living within your means. Are you rich? Do you like money? I certainly do. I knew to be very wise with spending every time this word was in rotation. That meant when I was in Walmart, I chose between two food items and did not pick both. Which one would last longer? Which meal could stretch? There was a method to it. Being frugal doesn't mean cheap, but it definitely does not mean "BALLIN!"

6. **Industry:** Lose no time; be always employed in something useful; cut off all unnecessary actions. Hard work. Proverbs 12:11 "He who tills his land will have plenty of bread, But he who pursues worthless things lacks sense." (NASB) When I hear this word, a line from 50 Cent's "Patiently Waiting" off *Get Rich or Die Tryin'* pops in my head. "These Industry (People) ain't friends, they know how to pretend!"

Never fails. This was the discipline that tied into how I approached new connections and relationships. It's very uncomfortable when life picks up quickly on your journey and you meet lots of new people. Not everyone is looking out for your best interests. Tons of people present themselves well, but have ill intentions. It's not our job to sort them out, but to achieve a dream, a goal, one must remain even keel. Don't get too high or too low off one conversation. Also, be wary of whom you share your ideas with. Business is business. No matter who it's with. It can be family, friends, wife, husband; people tend to do what they want to do and apologize later. I tend to be very idealistic, but every day I learn something new. Don't be fooled by kind words and handshakes. There are many I initially chose not to share this book with. It's better to let the work speak for you.

7. **Sincerity:** Use no hurtful deceit; think innocently and justly, and, if you speak, speak accordingly. The quality of being free from pretense, deceit or hypocrisy. Romans 12:9 "Let love be without hypocrisy Abhor what is evil; cling to what is good."

It's fitting this is the next word. There are tons of sincere and genuinely loving people. Those are the people whose encouragement helps on the bad days. But, for someone like me who has been called cocky and self-absorbed, it bothers me when someone questions my sincerity. I wouldn't say it if I didn't mean it. I would remain silent.

The week after May 29, 2019, I ran into an issue with someone who questioned my entire existence. This man posted on Facebook by starting off spelling my name incorrectly, "Aime (é) is attempting to work with our youth. He leeches off of other people's work to establish himself. He has no ethical compass. He has no business etiquette."

The irony is I read this message seconds after getting off a phone call with a mutual connection. I had called to attempt to discuss our disagreement. I didn't feel it was right for two African American men looking to help youth to have discord. When I was shown the message, I cried. It hurt deeply that someone would put false accusations into the atmosphere and question my sincerity. As you embark on the journey, you start to look back and see how the world moves. In every situation we can react or anticipate. Can't do both.

8. **Justice:** Wrong none by doing injuries, or omitting the benefits that are your duty. Just behavior or treatment. Psalm 106:3 "Blessed are those who act justly, who always do what is right."

You may be wondering if any justice came from that situation. One of that man's pupils reached out to me months later. I told him I'd love to meet with them both. No sense of burning the bridge. Back in June, I was considering relocating after living through weeks of hysteria. I didn't leave. And the justice that comes from both situations is you reading this right now. However you heard about it, and whether you saw me in person, on television or on your phone. I'm thankful to share this with you, and pray it will help you on your path.

9. **Moderation:** Avoid extremes; forbear resenting injuries so much as you think they deserve. Average in amount, intensity, quality or degree. Proverbs 25:27 "It is not good to eat much honey, nor if it is glorious to seek one's own glory." (NASB)

Drinking too much water can kill you. Don't overdo it. I overdid it with weed, alchohol and sex. These 13 virtues, steady discipline and some of the life shaking moments I've shared are what have helped me keep my mind on track. Actions, faith and constant repetition guide me.

We all are at war -- with our mirror, our spirit, our mind, and unfortunately with every other person on the planet. Choose your battles wisely.

10. **Cleanliness:** Tolerate no uncleanliness in body, clothes or habitation. The state or quality of being clean or being kept clean. Psalm 51:10 "Create in me a clean heart, O God, And renew a steadfast spirit within me." (NASB)

I judge women with this category. If you invite me to your home, and your bathroom and/or kitchen is not clean, I have zero interest in being anything more than friends. If you don't keep where you eat and bathe clean, how can you have a clean body? I love Pine-Sol. I hate dishes. There were many mornings I was late to meetings because I had to do the dishes before leaving. I can't cook if there are dishes in the sink. But, most importantly, understand how cleaning is therapeutic. It allows you to rock out to some music or even just think about a specific topic. You don't have to be as extreme as I am, but understand how cleanliness connects to your overall health and well-being.

11. Tranquility: Be not disturbed at trifles or at accidents common or unavoidable. Free from disturbance; calm. Hebrews 12:14 "Strive for peace with everyone, and for the holiness without which no one will see the Lord." (NASB)

Stop reading. Repeat aloud, "Tranquility" 10 times. Say it again. This time slower and with emphasis. Your entire body shifts. You feel better. It's a word that holds so much power because it allows you to embrace and appreciate whatever moment you're in. There are so many of us who never live a peaceful lifestyle because we don't deliberately practice it. Thoughts lead to feelings. Feelings lead to actions. Actions lead to results. If you want peace, think peace. Then make peaceful acts a part of your daily routine. Every time we get angry it's simply a reflection of an internal issue.

12. **Chastity:** Rarely use venery but for health or offspring, never to dullness, weakness, or the injury of your own or another's peace or reputation. The state or practice of refraining from extramarital, or especially from all, sexual intercourse. 1 Thessalonians 4:3 "For this is the will of God, your sanctification; that is, that you abstain from sexual immorality." (NASB)

In this book, I've opened up about how sexuality has impacted my life. It's been the driving force of my ego and the kryptonite to my success. I can't tell you how many times this popped up at a time where I was like a dog in heat. But abiding by it helped to keep everything else in line. For me this practice meant avoiding certain Instagram pages. It meant implementing self-control. I tried to run away from it, and yes, during those weeks I did not watch porn. It was about training my mind, body and spirit to fully be who I want to be remembered as. For some, this is a daunting task. Some of you may even be in a relationship where sex is the glue. I caution you, if it is, you're destined to fail. For me, sex was the pulse of every relationship I was in. As long as I "had her" there always was a connection. But, that's not right. The amount of times I received complaints and countered our conversation through seduction is embarrassing. There are many men who do this. And tons of women as well. I've gone on a bit of a tangent, but this system made me better.

13. **Humility:** Imitate Jesus and Socrates. A modest or low view of one's own importance; humbleness. Philippians 2:3 "Do nothing out of selfish ambition or vain conceit. Rather, in humility value others above yourselves." (NIV)

This word. Our society has a way of shaming confident people because of pompous individuals. This scripture is the best way to describe it. I grew up extremely competitive and driven by the idea of proving someone wrong. That's why I struggled so many times to be on the right path. The most eye-opening situation for me was in the Summer 2019 when I facilitated a group of 6th grade boys about Healthy Masculinity. At the close of each session we all shouted, "When you know what you stand for, you don't need to compete!" It melts my heart thinking about it.

Because to them, "Sir Aimézing" was someone who gets it. Someone who knows what it's like to be made fun of, to make fun of someone, and who feels acting cocky is the answer when scared. We do all things out of fear and love. Humility is a form of love. It's a form of showing appreciation and lowliness toward fellow humans. I'm extremely confident in my abilities to complete a task, but understanding that if a car hits me, or if I get cut, red blood comes out of me the same way it will you. In our world that thrives off separating and elevating, if there is anything I want you to take from these stories, it's that you are the only version of yourself.

There may be 7.8 billion people roaming the earth, but He only made one you. Take that with a humble heart, because there are many who didn't get a chance to be better. Many don't have the access to read a virtue. To me, being humble is making every day an opportunity to be a better human.

There are 52 weeks in a year. 13 total virtues, which means 4 times a year I dedicate and concentrate on each one of these words. Forcing the mind to lock in on such concepts evokes a new level of character building. But there's another part of the brain we want to get working.

It's our attitude. Here are a few concepts to implement daily.

1. **Enforce Self-Discipline:** This is what makes you think before you act. This is what allows your efforts to control your mind, personal initiative and positive mental attitude with enthusiasm.

2. **Control Your Enthusiasm:** Enthusiasm is more powerful than logic, reason, or rhetoric in getting your ideas across and in winning over others to your viewpoint. It is a state of mind. It inspires action and is the most contagious of all emotions.

3. **Think Accurately:** Accurate thinkers are the masters of their emotions. You must separate facts from information. Then separate facts into two classes: important and unimportant.

4. **Mastermind Alliance:** No individual has ever achieved success without the help and cooperation of others. A group of brains coordinated in a spirit of harmony will provide more thought energy than a single brain, just as a group of electric batteries will provide more energy than a single battery.

5. **Go the Extra Mile:** Strength and struggle go hand in hand. Render more and better service than you are paid for and sooner or later you will receive compound interest from your investment.

Then, there is the most important principle I've learned: Believe in yourself.

"Whatever the mind of man can conceive and believe, it can achieve."

– Napoleon Hill

THE
SHIFT

THE SHIFT

Take a deep breath and close your eyes.

Take 30-60 seconds and go to your most innocent and creative stage in life.

Maybe you were five years old playing outside or with your favorite toy.

Revisit when you had the most joy you ever felt.

Relive whatever was your most creative and pure state.

OPEN YOUR EYES

A study conducted by NASA in the 1970s stated our creativity level drops 68% between the ages of five and 15. We don't become less creative; we change due to learned behaviors.

"The opposite of courage in our society is not cowardice, it is conformity." (Rollo May, American Existential Psychologist)

Society forces roles on each and every single one of us. Boundaries are assigned to us by an envious and resentful world. The character you think you were born with is not who you are. We all inherit certain qualities, but parents, peers and friends tend to influence who we are and shape who we become.

"Your net worth is your network."

– Tim Sanders

Who ultimately controls this? You. Or will you continue to allow others to mold who you are? Every single one of us is an artist. Every single one of us is in business for ourselves. We are our brand, our most important asset.

What is success? There is no wrong answer. It is defined by the individual. You decide what success means to you. Not your significant other, sibling, mom, dad, friend, mentor, teacher…you.

"Success is the progressive realization of a worthy ideal."

– Earl Nightingale

"THE BIG 3"

"THE BIG 3"

Big 3? You mean Ice Cube's basketball league? The three great allied partners in World War II: Great Britain, The Soviet Union and The United States? Chocolate, vanilla and strawberry?

None of the above.

"Most folks are as happy as they make up their minds to be."

– Abraham Lincoln

People often say they want to be happy or successful, but they don't know how to do it. The "Big 3" is the first step towards achieving such. Let's start by the true definition of these terms. There is no such thing as happiness. There is only joy. Joy is defined as a feeling of great pleasure and happiness. Happiness is defined as a feeling of pleasure or contentment. See a similarity? We are really seeking pleasure. We are seeking a positive, enjoyable ecstasy.

A state of well-being, contentment, or pleasurable or satisfying experience all have one common trait. It is completely reliant on you. There is no secret juice, quote or idea that anyone else can create that will make you happy. It won't come from a relationship, like on a YouTube video or social media post. It won't come from people texting or snapping you all day. It won't come from a daily FaceTime. It will come from you. All the answers to your questions are already inside of you.

"Do you know what will happen to 100 individuals who start even at the age of 25 and who believe they will be successful? By the age of 65, only five out of 100 will make the grade! Why do so many fail? What happened to the sparkle that was there when they were 25? What became of their dreams, their hopes, their plans...and why is there such a large disparity between what these people intended to do and what they actually accomplished? That is...The Strangest Secret...We become what we think about. This is The Strangest Secret. Now, why do I say it's

strange and why do I call it a secret? Actually, it isn't a secret at all. It was first promulgated by some of the earliest wise men, and it appears again and again throughout the Bible. But very few people have learned it or understand it. That's why it's strange, and why for some equally strange reason it virtually remains a secret." (The Strangest Secret by Earl Nightingale)

"A man's life is what his thoughts make of it."

– Earl Nightingale

This curriculum is created to help you realize how special you truly are, just by being you. There is a one in a trillion chance that you were the sperm that connected with the egg through conception. Every single day there are babies that don't make it, and you've made it this far, so be thankful. Happiness is an attitude that we can control more than anything else.

Now take the time to seriously think about a few moments when you were happy. Those feelings had nothing to do with another person. Sure, someone may have been involved in the experience but when you get down to the nitty gritty, you were the most important factor.

"You create opportunity as you turn your crisis and defeat into success."

– Dennis Kimbro

Success -- the fact of getting or achieving wealth, respect or fame.

Every wealthy, respected, famous person that you can name started in their mother's womb just like you and me. A lot of people give the generic answer stating they want to be successful, but aren't willing to put forth the proper effort to truly become successful.

I want to applaud you for being among the few. The fact that you're reading this already shows that you're looking to become the greatest version of yourself.

"We've got to put the fuel in, before we can expect heat."

– Earl Nightingale

Success is simple but uncomfortable. Think about the past. In order to keep your family warm it required intense effort. You had to find a forest, cut down a tree, and then chop the logs into wood. After that strenuous process, you had to transport it back to your home. Then you had to put the wood in the fireplace before lighting the spark that started the fire.

This process can be applied to every single one of us, in every venture of life. Yet, circumstances will always differ. You may have to relocate to find a forest with better trees, the weather may play a factor, or there may be some people who were born in the forest and know exactly where to go. There may have been someone to point you in the direction when searching for a forest, but the common denominator will always be the actions we had to take in order to create heat.

A success can be a school teacher who is teaching because that's what they wanted to do. Or, it could be the owner of a gas station, a salesman, or an athlete. Anyone who took a worthy predetermined ideal and made it a reality because that's what they decided to deliberately. Only one out of 20 do this. Success is often measured by our esteem of each other by what we have, not by what we are.

"Society is a wave. The wave moves onward, but the water of which it is composed does not. The same particle does not rise from the valley to the ridge. Its unity is only phenomenal. The people who make up a nation today,

next year die, and their experience with them." (Emerson Essays Self-Reliance)

World-renowned comedian Kevin Hart has released tons of specials wherein he states, "Everyone wants to be famous, nobody wants to put the work in." Hart, a Philadelphia native, began his comedic career in 2001. Despite a number of feature films throughout the first decade of the new century, he did not reach stardom until 2011 when his stand-up special *Laugh at my Pain* grossed $15 million. This comedic film was the start of one of the most dominating runs by any American comedian, including becoming only the ninth comedian to sell out Madison Square Garden, not to mention starting his own production company, and utilizing social media platforms Instagram, Twitter and YouTube to enhance a remarkable resume. As you're reading this, Hart is releasing a new project whether it be film, YouTube or an upcoming tour.

Guarantee. Put the book down and ask Google real quick.

Welcome back!

What ultimately separates a successful and unsuccessful person is the drive within, the desire to achieve their goal. Malcolm Gladwell's *Outliers* touches on how resources and circumstances can impact us, but the award-winning author also mentions the 10,000 hour rule. This principle connects to the Laws of Nature, Karma, Reaping what you sow, etc., shows what we put in, and what we get out.

Success and happiness do run hand in hand, but the true connection is not the equivalency of money bringing contentment, but the role of self in accomplishing both. Nothing can bring you peace but yourself. Nothing can bring you peace but the triumph of principles. Do you have principles? Before starting any relationship, business or personal, values must be discussed.

Maybe we'll discuss this issue more in depth in a different book.

The Big 3 was created for multiple reasons. To identify:

The Problem: Recognize the different difficulties that get in the way of your goal, whether it be self, friends/family or distractions.

Produce and Consider Many Alternatives: Compile lists and quotes of ways to improve these areas in order to facilitate succeeding at goals.

Be Original: Each list is tailored specifically to that person. These lists can be created by all ages.

Get Glimpses of the Future: Talk about your progress. Example, if a student has a goal of having a car, track going out to eat less and taking fewer Ubers as they press toward their goal.

Visualize the Inside: The moment the goal is written down, the image is created in the mind. "Visualize before you actualize."

Enjoy and Use Fantasy: Who do you admire? Who inspires you? Do they have more than 24 hours in a day?

Elaborate-But Not Excessively: This is more along the lines of identifying the problems standing in the way, and creating strategies to overcome them.

The Big 3 was created to assist in the structuring of balanced success. It is a way of analyzing self while setting goals, that through daily repetition, become reality via proficient practice. In order to fully embrace and achieve the advancement of what this book provides, you must drill the aforementioned quotes into your mind.

Our minds are like soil. What you plant will blossom. If you put a little poison in a vegetable garden, it inevitably will spread. The vibrations of our minds are connected to the words we say and the deeds we do, but the most powerful keys are the thoughts we create. As we begin this journey together, I recommend you keep notes on your phone or on a notepad so you maximize every piece of knowledge and wisdom that will be shared.

"He cannot be happy and strong until he, too, lives with nature in the present, above time."

– Ralph Waldo Emerson

ONE THING YOU LIKE TO DO

ONE THING YOU LIKE TO DO

Grab a pen. Grab paper. Right now. Write down one thing you enjoy doing, and wish you could do around the clock 24/7 non-stop. Doesn't matter what it is. Defer judgement. Keep in mind, this is for you, written by you. It never has to be shared with any other individual.

Don't be lazy. If you're the type who doesn't like to do anything, then you need to reread the last chapter. We all have a hobby or passion. Maybe you like to have sex. There are millions of people who do. And that's okay. Sex is powerful and people with a high sex drive often possess the ability to reach the highest points on the ladder of success. Just be alert that power can also work against you. Overindulgence of sex can destroy the power of will and lead to the habit of drifting. Sex can be transmuted into the driving force capable of lifting one to great heights of achievement. The problem most people run into is inability to have mastery over self and caution. Sex is one of those hobbies that when we really like it, we seem to act without thinking or planning before we act. It's a natural desire, but it can change your life, responsibilities and the people around you, forever.

Enough sex talk, let's talk about why a hobby is important. It is a scientific fact that people have died due to boredom. It's also a fact that death naturally is most humans' biggest fear. We are all designed to preserve ourselves and adapt for survival. This is shown in religious and scientific studies. Don't believe me, again we can discuss it with our friend Google. And if you want to really go deeper, I recommend you research Rollo May and read some of his studies on mankind as a whole.

Back to the first part of the "Big 3" What is the one thing you like to do? When you wrote it down, did you smile on the inside? Did you smile even writing it down because your brain took you to the place of emotion that evokes the sense of appreciation that fills you while you're doing it? It's remarkable how the mind and body can create sensations simultaneously just off a word or thought.

"Turn your work into fun. Make what you have to do into something you want to do."

– Sir Aimézing

Starting off your "Big 3" with something you like to do is essential because it's personalizing and reassuring at the same time. You don't have to train your mind or force yourself to focus on something you already enjoy. Think about it from this perspective. By putting forth the effort and focus on achieving your goals, you are creating more time to do what you enjoy. Simple enough right? I can recall the episode of the *Chappelle Show,* 'Making Da Band' when Dave Chapelle, impersonating Diddy, went on a spiel about what he would prefer doing all day. And it included having sex, going to the movies and singing songs. Obviously this was an exaggeration for comedic reasons, so let's focus on the more important elements. What he liked to do was something he liked and it didn't matter how anyone felt about it. Because when and if he had time to do it, he could do it!

Hobbies are done in leisure time and for pleasure. You have every right to enjoy yourself however you'd like to, as long as it does not violate the rights of our fellow civilians. Identifying one thing that you like to do is a warm up to get the brain flowing in a positive state.

Disclaimer: If you write something down that causes you to have anxiety or stress, it's an issue. Either you enjoy your pain and need to seek deeper guidance to unlock yourself from such a state of mind, or you truly don't enjoy the act. It's okay. We are all conditioned to feel there are things that we "should" like to do. Keep it simple and honest. Write down what you like to do.

Doing what we like to do ultimately enables us to become more productive. It engages us and creates more dedication. Motivation to do what we like to do always gives an extra jolt of energy. When I was a kid, I always did my chores quicker during the summer.

1. There was more time because there was no school.
2. There was more sunlight, which meant more time for basketball.

Think about a child who likes to play videogames. When mom or dad disturb him, he rushes to get done what his parents need so he can get back to playing the game. Doing what we like to do, is what makes us better leaders. There's a level of tranquility that these avocations establish.

ONE THING
YOU WANT
TO IMPROVE

ONE THING YOU WANT TO IMPROVE

Okay, this is where it gets fun. The number of people who have looked me in the face and said, "Nothing," is comical. If there is no way you can improve anything in your life, put this book down. DM me on Instagram and tell me your secret! I want to meet your friends, family, significant others, so we can talk in depth on how they can help make me perfect.

There is always room to improve, whether from a physical, mental or spiritual perspective. I'll list a few ways we all can improve:

1. **Family** - Do you find that during quality time your face is buried in your phone whether it be Amazon, E-Trade, your email, Facebook, Tik Tok, etc.? Are you addicted to swiping and liking on a mobile device? Well, you can improve it. To close out 2019, I enabled the screen time tracking option on my phone and set limits for all social media apps that come at 10:45 pm. Of course, I can check an Instagram story at 10:47 pm, but at least there are words that make me reconsider and send waves to my brain saying, "It's not that serious, sir!"

2. **Health** - There are tons of dietary apps, social media pages, trainers, fitness enthusiasts, etc. all

accessible on the same phone we discussed using less. Ask your doctor, ask a trainer, ask a nutritionist! Do you ever wonder why your body doesn't feel right after a meal? Maybe it's because you don't eat for the right reasons. Health can also mean going to the gym, walking at the park, or even investing in a Nintendo switch so you can put yourself in the best possible situation. Exercise produces both physical and mental buoyancy. It clears sluggishness and dullness from the body and mind.

3. **Health Part II -** This is a layered category. Are you in unhealthy relationships, romantic and/or platonic that ultimately prevent you from maximizing your abilities? Sometimes, we are the problem. It could stem from our inability to communicate, be open, and be vulnerable.

"Lions hang with Lions, Iron sharpens Iron."

– Sir Aimézing

You have never seen a lion hang out with a hyena, not even in Disney films. We often get so emotionally connected to people we put their desires before our own. That's unhealthy. In order to love someone, you have to love yourself. And there is no love being presented when we keep ongoing toxic connections flowing. No individual has achieved success without the help and cooperation of others. The value of gathering together those of a like mind is self-evident. Think of a group of batteries -- a group of minds will provide more energy, only if they're aiming for the same result. There is no record of any great contribution to civilization without the cooperation of others.

Finances - More money doesn't equate to more bliss. This is deeper than that though. Finances can mean improving your credit score, saving more, reviewing your monthly bank statements to see why and how are you still living check to check. It could mean stocks, life insurance, IRAs -- anything that has to do with capital.

Personal - If you picked up this book, that means you realize there is something going on inside of you that is not working at the highest level of efficiency. Confidence, Focus, Belief. There are so many different ways to take this. Remember this is a list to help you. And only you know the real you.

Those are a few ways to go, and if you still feel like you are the Alpha and Omega, then ask someone you trust what your weaknesses are. We often have a tainted view of our true abilities, that's why it's so vital to have the right people around when we are looking to become better humans. There are people who love to "gas" up others, and while they're heaping on the praise, they're actually preparing to watch you burn up in flames.

Example: You have a friend who has been doing music for more than seven years but can't catch a break. Are you a real friend if you share her music but never listen to it? Don't get me wrong, support is vital, but if the album is horrible, shouldn't you say so? Couldn't this be another option to improve? Maybe the real question is: How do I communicate more honestly with the people I love?

Improving is often associated in a negative way, and falls in line with our six biggest fears. Every person on earth is afraid of something.

Fear of Poverty
Fear of Death
Fear of Old Age
Fear of Loss of Love
Fear of Poor Health
Fear of Criticism

When you analyze those fears, I'm sure you can come up with one thing to improve on. Because we all can improve in each category. Plus, the information era allows us access to solutions to every fear!

I've already said my mom is my hero and I love her with all my heart. Her drive inspires me daily, but even though she has a laptop and a phone, she still asks me questions as if my name is Google and not Sir Aimézing. I can't be the only millennial who has had the, "Mom, I don't know, Google exists," conversation. Doesn't that make it even more apparent for us all to utilize our resources?

Refusing to use resources is like us being inhabitants of the earth and not using water. Our bodies are mostly made of water. We can go without food for extended periods of time as long as we have water. Water keeps us clean. Water for most of human existence was the most consistent and reliable use of transporting goods. Water is used for various reasons in multiple religions.

Water is needed for the growth of every essential natural bred product.

ONE GOAL FOR THE END OF THE YEAR

ONE GOAL FOR THE END OF THE YEAR

No this isn't a New Year's Resolution. It's a goal that can take longer than a year, or it might take three weeks. It's been said it takes 21 days to break a habit. But there's more. The only way to break a bad habit is to create a new habit. Read that again. And again. And again. How many times do people bang their heads against the wall not understanding how they keep slipping up? Your mind is like the earth rotating; it does not stop. So, to overcome or shift your behavior, you have to replace it with better behavior. All things are matter made of atoms and to use this to our benefit, certain actions must be taken. All your successes and failures are results of the habits you have formed.

"We have to put the fuel in before we can expect heat." Your goal is heat. And if you don't put forth the process of finding the forest, cutting down the tree, chopping the wood, transporting it, and then loading the fireplace, you won't get heat. It's really a simple concept.

What separates people is goals. Some of us have goals, some of us don't. When you have a goal, your mind subconsciously will put you in position to capitalize on that goal.

"Throw your heart over the bar and your body will follow."

— Norman Vincent Peale

Write down your goals. It is the first step of your blueprint. Success and progress towards achieving your goals in life begin with knowing where you are going. It is better to act on a plan that is still in development than to delay acting at all. Personal initiative is contagious. It succeeds where others fail; it creates work, opportunity, the future, and advancement. Personal initiative is the inner power that starts all action.

Think about being on a ship. A ship starts at the dock or harbor. When passengers get on, it's unclear how they will get to the destination. That's what the captain's job is. The captain and crew have a blueprint or plan. Even though it's unclear upon departure, there is an exact process mapped out to arrive at the final location. Every single one of us is the captain of our own ship. Are you going to be someone without a plan just hoping to make it to shore? Or are you going to take control?

"The man on top of the mountain didn't fall there."

— Vince Lombardi

We all have the ability to climb. All we need is to choose our mountain, and then map out the plan to climb.

What separates the successful from the failures? Goals. We are the captains of our own ships. Every captain and crew have a map, designed to arrive at the ultimate destination. Without a goal, you're a person at sea, waiting for the boat to flip. Goals are what empower the idea of discipline, self-control, and decision-making. When a goal is on your mind, you're motivated to stay on task.

"Go as fast you can but never hurry."

– Sir Aimézing

Reread the last page.

Goal - The object of a person's ambition or effort; an aim or desired result. What is your true desire? What is your true purpose? How many times have we made the excuse, "One thing led to another." It is a lie! Every single action the body performs was first a thought. Every single action. When you cheated on your ex, you thought about it a bunch of times before it happened. The situation most likely didn't just present itself and you seized it. Have you ever seen a social media post from someone who shares a picture or video of a couple in a gym, and they write, "Relationship Goals," but the person who shared it never even goes to the gym! How can that be a goal if you do nothing to make it a reality? Think about Thomas Edison. It took him 10,000 tries to perfect the electric light bulb. But, in whatever room you're reading this, the lights won't turn on by themselves.

Are you willing to hit the switch? Are you willing to get up and take the necessary steps? A journey of 1,000 miles starts with the first step.

FEAR

The demons in your head are dead.

Don't let them live.

Yesterday is gone, but tomorrow awaits.

Why live in fear?

Here today, gone tomorrow

We all are destined to die.

Don't cry when I go.

Be a better you.

There are voices in my head full of discouragement.

Mute them.

We only live once so, "Live it up"

Don't be stupid.

Mistakes prepare us for success.

What ideas do we lose, when we're stupid?

How hungry can you be when your back is against the
wall?

You ever been unemployed, behind on bills and the IRS
take all of your taxes?

You ever made $45 in five hours moving furniture?

You ever asked your girlfriend for money to buy weed for you to smoke?

You ever crashed your car in the snow, while drunk?

The story of fear.

That's why Eve and Adam hesitated when He spoke to them.

That's why our parents stay married and unhappy for the sake of "the kids"

Why fear?

Man walked on the moon.

Created a car.

Flew a plane.

Became the president.

Two eyes.

Two ears.

One mouth.

Two legs.

Two feet.

"The more you learn, the more you realize you don't know. The more effective you'll become."

— Albert Einstein

WHY FEAR?

At some point in time people begin to think that learning stops. That is absolutely untrue. Learning should take place every day. It doesn't matter if you're Frank Lucas or Albert Einstein, both lacked something. Oh, you don't like the reference to two geniuses who ran into limitations? The point is there is no human alive today or from the past who knew everything there was to know. David was one of the wisest Biblical figures and even though he knew Bathsheba was the wife of another man, he still needed to learn what his actions really meant.

For those who may not know all the details of David's story, here is a quick recap. A prophet was sent to share a story to open David's eyes after he had Bathseba's husband killed in war. David committed adultery, even though he was a heroic figure. He may have defeated Goliath, but still had to improve.

Now, take your pen and write down what you need to improve. Don't beat yourself up. Just one thing. It's called "The Big 3" for a reason. Rome wasn't built in a day. You have to crawl before you walk. And for those who doubt their ability to walk, just remember every walking human once was a struggling infant, tumbling over back and forth, grabbing onto walls and tables around them. Every crawling baby watched his parents and other big people move around at free will thinking "Hey! I want to move without your help!" That same drive and determination we possessed in our innocence of youth can be awakened in our present self.

PROMISE TO YOURSELF

PROMISE TO YOURSELF

Challenge yourself. Read this oath from Napoleon Hill's *Law of Success* daily. This isn't a book. This is an introduction to a lifestyle. The choice is yours.

"I know that I have the ability to achieve the object of my definite purpose. Therefore I demand of myself persistent, aggressive and continuous action towards it attainment.

I realize that the dominating thoughts of my mind will eventually reproduce themselves in outward bodily action. And gradually transform themselves into physical reality. Therefore I will concentrate my mind 30 minutes daily upon the task of thinking of the person I intend to be. By creating a mental picture of this person, and then transforming that picture into reality through practical service.

I know through the principle of Autosuggestion any desire I persistently hold in my mind will eventually seek expression through some practical means of realizing it. Therefore I will devote 10 minutes daily to the development of the necessary principles in order to achieve such.

I have clearly mapped out and written down a description of my definite purpose in life for the coming five years. I have set a price on my services for each of these five years, a price I intend to earn and receive through strict application of the principle of efficient, satisfactory service which I will render in advance.

I fully realize that no wealth or position can long endure unless built upon truth and justice; therefore I will engage in no transaction which does not benefit all humans. I will succeed by attracting to me the forces I wish to use and the cooperation of other people. I will induce others to serve me, because I will first serve them. I will eliminate hatred, envy, jealousy, selfishness and cynicism by developing a love for all humanity. Because I know that a negative attitude toward others can never bring me success. I will cause others to believe in me, because I believe in them and in myself. I will sign my name to this formula, commit it to memory, and repeat it aloud once a day with full faith that it gradually influences my entire life so that I will become a successful and joyous being in my choice of endeavor."

END

Everyone is a hero. Even when we don't know it. There was a student who shared with me how she talked a peer out of committing suicide. Her friend struggled with loving himself and felt he had no worth. I looked her in the eyes, and said, "You're a hero." If you help one person or save one life, you are a hero. My story and my journey is one of billions of people who have faced tribulations. You have your own. You are writing it at this very moment. I may not be everyone, and you may not know it, but you are a hero and I love you.

ABOUT THE AUTHOR

Aimé Mukendi, Jr. aka Sir Aimézing is a motivational speaker, life coach, social media influencer, entrepreneur, radio show host, blogger and author. He is President of The Shift & Crew, LLC, a SkoVu TV Show host, and President of Morningstar Miracles Foundation, Inc. He has received many awards including an award from the Changemakers 30 Under 30 awards. The annual awards event honors some of the most prolific and dynamic young professionals from the Western New York region.

Sir Aimézing is a public speaker that inspires audiences across the globe. He is an in-demand speaker for executives, salespeople, educators, community leaders, and other professionals. He advises clients in New York and nationally. He is featured in broadcast and national media. Sir Aimézing speaks at virtual events, conferences, and events nationally.

To have Sir Aimézing speak or host an upcoming event, or to promote your brand, or for more information on Sir Aimézing, visit: **https://siraimezing.com**

For more information on his blog, and a few Aimézing Words, visit: **https://blogs.siraimezing.com**

Follow Sir Aimézing on Facebook, Instagram, Twitter and YouTube: @**SirAimezing**

Made in the USA
Columbia, SC
06 July 2020

13194708R00074